AND MORNING

And morn- ing

Poems by
Roland Flint

Dryad Press

Washington, D.C. & San Francisco

ACKNOWLEDGEMENTS

Some of these poems first appeared in the following publications:
*The Atlantic Monthly, Dacotah Territory, Dryad, Film Heritage, Equal Time,
George Mason Review, Minnesota Review, Poetry Northwest, Plainsong,
Proteus, Salmagundi, South Dakota Review, and Woodwind.*

This writing was supported in part by a Discovery Grant in 1970 from the National
Endowment for the Arts.

LIBRARY OF CONGRESS CATALOGING IN PUBLICATION DATA

Flint, Roland.

And Morning.

I. Title.

PS3556.L56A8   811'.5'4   74-11608

Published by:

DRYAD PRESS

P. O. Box 1656   2943 Broderick Street
Washington, D.C. 20013   San Francisco, CA 94123

CONTENTS

Skin

I dedicate this book to my children,
Elizabeth Fitzgerald Flint
Ethan David Flint (1966-1972)
and Pamela Helen Flint

SKIN

If the wood is good grain,
and the carpenter, the fit, the caulking,
the cask will be good
and if the grapes are good
the wood and the wine
will improve each other,
in the dark long days of aging.

The separate tastes of earth
will taste again and change again each other,
until, like membrane, somehow
in and between the wood and wine
there will be no separation,
wood from dark from wine.

When this goes on, anything can happen.
Go back, go back to mystery.
Now I am grateful to my small poem
for teaching me this again:
that my God is still the moment
where the wood is no longer itself,
where the wine is no longer, only, itself.

I

FOLLOW

Now here is this man mending his nets
after a long day, his fingers
nicked, here and there, by ropes and hooks,
pain like tomorrow in the small of his back,
his feet blue with his name, stinking of baits,
his mind on a pint and supper—nothing else—
a man who describes the settled shape
of his life every time his hands
make and snug a perfect knot.

I want to understand, if only for the story,
how a man like this,
a man like my father in harvest,
like Bunk Mac Vane in the stench of lobstering,
or a teamster, a steelworker,
how an ordinary working stiff,
even a high tempered one,
could just be called away.

It's only in one account
he first brings in a netful—
in all the others, he just calls,
they return the look or stare and then
they 'straightaway' leave their nets to follow.
That's all there is. You have to figure
what was in that call, that look.

(And I wouldn't try it on a tired working man
unless I was God's son—
he'd kick your ass right off the pier.)

If they had been vagrants,
poets or minstrels, I'd understand that,
men who would follow a different dog.
But how does a man whose movement,
day after day after day,
absolutely trusts the shape it fills
put everything down and walk away?

I'd pass up all the fancy stunting
with Lazarus and the lepers
to see that one.

EARTHWORM

I think of a girl who hated to walk in the rain,
loathing to step on them. I hope she got over that.
We liked to keep one on the sidewalk
and line it up with another
for an excruciating race,
or to put it back in the grass
and watch its progress. Burrowing.

We said, when he's underground,
and worming, the earth goes right through him.

I still think of him that way, lank, blind,
both ends open, refining whatever comes,
dirt among rose roots, yeasty bodies.

He doesn't look for trouble. He just follows warmth,
at the earth's curve, coming up only for rain
and the feet of girls.

AUGUST FROM MY DESK

It is hot today, dry enough for cutting grain,
and I am drifting back to North Dakota
where butterflies are all gone brown with wheat dust.

And where some boy,
red-faced, sweating, chafed,
too young to be dying this way,
steers a laborious, self-propelled combine,
dreaming of cities, and blizzards—
and airplanes.

With the white silk scarf of his sleeve
he shines and shines his goggles,
he checks his meters, checks his flaps,
screams contact at his dreamless father,
he pulls back the stick,
engines roaring,

and hurtles into the sun.

ICTHUS

A thousand bushel of herring—
for sardines—sucking up through
a vacuum hose a foot in diameter,
shooting down into room sized holds,
furious, orgasmic, with life or losing it,
and ten minutes later
in layers of rough salt
they are all dead,
all the ones on top,
and I think if one is alive in there
when they get back to the cannery
and the women begin to cut
that it will be the son of Christ.

TURN

When I lie under the tall trees
at this time of year,
no leaves yet but the buds ready to break,
when the separate winds make whole branches
move drift return sway,
I see every possible thing is here,
from the first stir of creation
to the slow unwinding hieratic floods,
branches the shapes of grief or expectation,
infantile and ancient in the same knot,
branches naked as roots.

And I dream the branches into roots—
turn the worlds around,
try to imagine in what underground sea,
in what floating skies of humus
the rooted branches drift, dreaming,
into what clouds of anthracite they stare,
the sea weed branches waved into the nitrogen silent water.

It makes me believe again
in mirror versions of the universe—
somewhere another poet writing this,
lying on his back facing the lovely
unchanging secret at the center,
wondering the other world, dreaming
his dream of me.

EARLY CUTTING
For Ed Elderman

When they take the winter wheat at home
all the other crops are green.
In granaries and tight truck boxes
farm boys are slow scoop-shovel metronomes
singing harvest deep in the grain.

The old men come out to watch, squat in the stubble,
break a lump of dirt and look at it on their hands,
and mumbling kernels of the sweet hard durum,
they think how it survived the frozen ground
unwinding at last to this perfect bread
of their mouths.

Where they call it the Red River Valley of the North
there are no mountains,
the floor is wide as a glacial lake—Agassiz,
the fields go steady to the horizon,
sunflower, potato, summerfallow, corn,
and so flat that a shallow ditch
can make tractor drivers think of Columbus
and the edge.

MEMENTO

When you make a coat of me
you'll need to lengthen the sleeves,
my arms are short, the hands already gone,
from felt to baize to nothing—rubbed away,
you'll have to add the lace, and pockets,
stitch some emblem on the breast,
with a legend—anything
except death before dishonor will do,
cut the legs off at the knees,
and put me on, take me off,
hang me up and say to anyone,
it's not a great coat (and it may be)
but it's a good coat, it will do.
I got it from the poet Flint,
second hand but serviceable.
Try it on—it fits almost anyone.
At first look you wouldn't see the reds
so of course it's gray—they were miners
in Wales, West Virginia, Indiana,
farmers in North Dakota, gray, a little dull.
But he said you'll find the red blood coat
of the living man, I promise,
if you remember—and wear it well.

HOME MADE

The red huge woman
stands close to the pot
her belly big
stirring stirring soap
mess of lye and ashes

red hand
the split board stir
over heat
her shoulders loped
haunches from behind

she looks as if she's
stirring her
self she is

stirring soap
mess of lye and
ashes

ELEGY

In North Dakota, when she died,
My uncle chewed his fist and cried.

Putting cousins and hogs to rout
He damned my aunt for playing out

And hid behind a roughage bin
Slugging his sorrow full of gin.

That night, dead drunk, his grief gone lame,
He found *exactly* what's to blame:

"It's not the world itself but all
The bastards . . . *ah.*" I watched him fall

Under the booze, under the moon.
I won't forget his anger soon.

PRAYER, POOR SINNERS, HOMELY GIRLS

Father today I forgave that sinner myself his pain
for the homely girls hoodwinked and left,
for heavy girls crying the goodbye boy
did lay them down in small time pastures,
for the wide nosed farmers' daughters
who swung like lonely cows in town
and there were milked, stripped, and left,
again, to brood and ruminate.

Yes I forgive him Father your pain of his past
as may please God the girls
and thrive.

WIFE AND BROTHER

Tonight three gulls fell from the moon
To gauge like gods the perfect waves,
And as you dream after your run
Above the sea, that flying moves

Me back. I hear the formal cries
At church, I watch a steeple spear
The sun, I feel the loss
Brought home, and I try not to stare.

They send us out to play because
Dividing the farm gets rough and we
Are kids. Free, David flies
Before my fear, so I fly too.

The old man's water spaniels know
He's dead and moan at winds. Our dog
Climbs with us to the mow
Where David squeals when I play pig.

Then back inside he laughs, "the sky
Is falling on the barn, a cloud
Is on its back," and I
Blush, guilty, when the uncles scold.

Old relatives who comfort death
Forgive us pagans as young fools,
But David's only faith
Was always blood, its jags and falls.

And here tonight when sea wind caught
Your hair and laced your feet with foam
You were the grace that taught
Me joy again and brought me home.

Warm with the smells of salt and sand,
Nakedness I can touch, you sleep
My love. I catch your dreaming hand
And David scatters dancing sheep.

DEAD FRIEND

John Kondos used to scale the tops of girders
on bridges, singing *South of the Border,* in Greek,
he clawed at stars, dead drunk and unafraid.

Five foot six, he picked fights
with goliaths in bars and never won
but still through stubs of teeth
he smiled and sang.

Once he stole roses from a funeral home
and gave them to a girl . . .
and went to jail.

They kicked him out of the army, of course,
for deserting, which he always did.

On the way home from Leavenworth
he rammed a trailer truck head on.
And now,
"God's will," the priest assures himself,
transplanted Greeks mourn to unfamiliar sounds,
"horrible," "too young," "accident, accident."

John Kondos knew what he was doing
every minute.

SHE WAS EIGHT

Patsy Murphy had red knuckles
from marble games
and went coatless in winter,
early and late.

When she died
we went to see her
in her inevitable pink coffin,
and tried to think of missing her.
I envied the Catholics, busy with their hands.
She was eight.

Now is a time
of crippled sounds through the soft air,
of doves making summer grief,
of leghorns flapping anger at the sky.

Here on the prairie, our dream of ocean,
we can see the sun all day,
and watch the moon stand up,
flowers open, flowers close.

No flower, nothing delicate . . .
implicit in her features, all too large,
was beauty,
her grudging fudging marble skill
said woman, strong.

In reluctant prairie trees outside
the grass makes small obeisance to a stream
that is reaching for the sea,
leaves cartwheeling on its back,
while minutely speckled minnows sweep
silently, and swift as gulls.

My face is growing smaller.

Patricia my classmate has been dead
for twenty years.

HIS GOOD TIME

Where is his mind, the old Greek farmer at the bar?
His son and young wife stand, while he sits,
drinking from the bottle with closed lips.
They know he's crazy, and mugging they tell the bartender,
who is looking up from the glass the old man shoved away.
He doesn't speak, but he buys the round.

They flank him and watch the coin purse unpuckering,
when he squeezes it, like something obscene.
Crazy, but he holds the money and knows amounts.
Therefore do his kin stand ready, contemptuous,
but patient, as he presses his index finger to his ear,
his cheek, his nose, or holds it up and looks
at it, smiling, sucking his beer and humming.

He dreams the footpaths in Crete,
the contrition of a young wife, her head held so,
the caves of the sea at night, his catechism,
a son born in a cave of sod, the endless earth of North Dakota
the clapboard rising at last . . . in the sea,
the blade breaking into new ground, his ground,
into . . . her head held so, his last wife.
And she stands patient now
as he presses his ear, cheek, nose,
or hums to his finger a vague falsetto,
deeds, documents and unforgiveables
with the coin purse in his breast.

They've known his mind is gone since they found him,
in the cold night, wearing only his long johns,
a pitchfork in his hands, cleaning the barn in the dark.
They watched him and laughed with relief,
the old man grinning back and nodding emptily.
But he surprised them by keeping a hard clear place
for the money, paying bills in cash, not speaking.

This is his good time, out of hurt but in charge,
before someone whispers power of attorney.
And someone will.

But what did their faces do
the first time they tried to take him
and he blazed up clutching that coin purse—
Odysseus, crazy, dressed like a bum
and stringing the bow.

BACK FROM WHEREVER

This pup is spooky,
looks right *at* me—
like he wants to know.
Staring.

I know it's stupid
but I get him alone,
looking back,
and whisper
Rilke? Buber?
He wags, smiles—ah
Roethke.

All right—he isn't Roethke.
But he might be:
rattle assed, dancing,
slug nutty in the leaves,
crapping in the garden,
never the luck in a small skin bag
and back already.

RICH

Being rich is your own mountain
up there in the soft dollar clouds that rain
in the pure sun
old twenty dollar gold pieces
foundations in Inca blood
in gold the color of an old prospector's blood
the one who wore out fifteen mules
before he became your father's father
patron of the arts
and stayed up there to build your house
which has in the east wall
the place of shrines
a window aperture that once a day
the new red sun comes into
like twenty dollar blood.

From one window all Los Angeles
from another the San Fernando Valley
crawling up the slopes in disarray
the bones of a thousand mules
outfitted to last:
prospectors, sun worshippers, your descendants—
see them, watch them come.

PREACHERS

God is the prayer which never fails
of a presence he finds in his mouth
every time it opens on your hurt
and he fetches in there
for something to say:
in the late innings he'd call it
reaching back for
a little something extra—pull the string.

That's why he's so patient about disaster
your brother's death or his—
he just opens his mouth
and there is that parabola
draining into peace along his chin.

There is no vanity in it:
when it comes out perfect
he calls it God.

This shouldn't sound as if
I think he's deluded,
as if I know what he's all about:
I wish to speak peace to you,
peace to the preacher, peace
to the funny shapes in his face,
peace to the God who puts them there or not.

SHAMPOO

Drubbing my fingers above my ears
suddenly for the first time
I'm really feeling my head,
a big round bone and I can't quite
get my hands around it.
It's the size of a big coconut,
but not symmetrical,
like a small winter squash,
knobbed and ridged like that.
Upright and plugged it would hold
half a liter of beer—I hope it will some day.
Now it's filled with cliffs, clefts, poems,
rivers of incredible girls
and long red slides.
It seems to me to be a good hard head.
And I can't quite get my hands around it.

POEM BEGINNING & ENDING O
for the cast & crew of "The Exorcist"

O
it was wonderful when
the movies (the makers) came to school,
o it was ivy xmas beverly all the way,
yes it was fibre glass and many special lights,
central casting at the Marriott Motel,
and yes sir starlets like Danish pastry frosted,
still glamorous, still cinemamorous
beneath the layers, and layers,
and when they closed the streets with a
"sizable cash donation,"
to the DC police club for delinquent boys,
and when, for scholarships in a
"large but undisclosed amount,"
they bought the campus—yard, lock,
and flying buttresses—
when they screwed the virgin blondes
for bit and two line speaking parts,
did another take on day,
and had the campus clergy
saying mass and eating Christ on cue O
(and when we saw at last how much we loved it—*we loved it*)
it was then we knew
they really know
what dreams are all about
O

HIGH SCHOOL HOCKEY IN MINNESOTA

These slow men from the Iron Range—
how they laugh
watching their clean sons skate.

SWORD & SHEATH

1. Many ancients, Sophocles, Lucretius,
have called the thighs' rich loam
a place to plow—or war.

2. Some Puritan ladies wore a certain belt
and from it down their downy bellies hung
a long forbidding cylinder
into the top of which was put
an ornamental bodkin
bare and wood.

3. To the wronged lady, Bergman's hero says
I bare my chest to your knife as you opened your legs
to the blade of my love.

4. A girl gives me a stiletto, for letters,
called Excalibur, saying
There's nothing Freudian
and my wife says
Keep it at the office.

5. Plowshare furrow scabbard sword,
wounded wounding as language man,
old as planting and penetration,
metaphors to the quick
warm satin sheath.
Vagina sounds like a mill
(Vagina Mill & Elevator), or brewery,
and Cunt sounds like a quiver:
Clytemnestra's.

FREEFALL

Falling free I know
there is nothing between what I am
and where I'm going
except this handle, lanyard
and paraffin of nylon streamers
My knuckles stop with thought
that doesn't want to rip it
Silence is part of the slowness
and there wouldn't couldn't be a crash—
I'd just dream into it,
the green wide mow of the valley,
my life below my eyes, my past
above stones of the head I'm tied to,
life taking the ground a mile
before the thud I won't even feel or hear,
or hitting a ricochet shot,
to move in space beyond,
to float falling free with no parachute,
canopy, streamers, ripcord.

IV

GHOST

Up here I keep the ones I'm doing,
in this drawer the ones I've done,
here the ones for now beyond me,
and way down here the unfinished
or broken ones that won't fit
anywhere—in a drawer I open only
to put things *in*.

But now and then
something gets out by itself and limps
patched and haggard to stand by my bed
where he clears his throat
like an alchemist
trying to make a good impression.
So I pretend I'm sleeping.

He just rocks back and forth a little,
glancing from his chewed up nails to me,
then staring at the floor, waiting.

And pretty soon there we are again,
both our ragging heads in the lamp,
arguing like friendly Jews,
a little here a little there.

INDIANS ARE BAD DRINKERS

The drunk man in the new hat is red,
or darker, the permanent corner
slurring among our blondes.
And aborigines drink badly in Australia,
in New Zealand the Maoris, where shadows of them,
darker, the mori-oris, who ate insects and honey,
were so black that nobody drinks like that.

But every light skin needs a drunken Indian
to lug around the dark it fears
to give strong drink to:
so he can drink without a worry—
he won't get drunk . . . some Indian will.

And sure enough, some Indian will,
in a new hat, wild and drunk
in Sioux Falls on Saturday night,
with a knife in his hand.

Because why not?
Indian is as Indian does
and does it right up here in front
to be himself for him—and for me too.

(Will you have just a taste, Mr. Hyde?—
I wouldn't if I were you)

Listen: the Little Big Horn was a whiskey jug,
those crazy bastards were drunk,
killing themselves killing us—and
they didn't sober up till Wounded Knee.

In Minnesota tonight the beautiful Scandinavians
are drinking a river of beer and aquavit:
a red man in an old hat
sits naked in his dug-out,
the dark sun
dark along his spine.
He's going nowhere away,
but always inland
to sow and blossom white.

HEADS OF THE CHILDREN

"If a son shall ask bread of any of you . . . . "

Father your voice was a fist
to slam my stomach shut
to start me from sleep like a rat,
you were the right and righteous anger,
your voice made me believe
in God in the Devil.

When we meet now, forty and seventy,
you are apologetically quiet,
you put your arms around me
and I know you mean it.
We are both old men.

But I can only remember
being held by you during beatings,
which were not often but terrible,
and always worse, before them,
the fanatical white in your shouting.
I know, now, you didn't mean it.

But listen to me—
I'm doing the same thing
to my small son.
If my voice said what I mean
he could sleep all night in its branches,
but I hear your outrage in me,
over nothing, a bare lie, or nothing,
and I see him cower for the storm cellar,
just like me, his knuckles white with my yelling.
Father—I love you.
Jesus Christ, where does it end?

POEM

At last I have entered welcome
and touched the metaphor of welcome
to find myself healthy and strong as I thought.
The yearning doesn't stop,
but now I know there is enough
and I am worthy.

Soon I'll be forty years old
and I am broken, permanently,
in some ways I did not devise
and may not speak of.

But now there is a hurt ended,
because someone, without righteousness,
has welcomed me,
and it only has to happen once.

I think there should be something here
that has a harpsichord
or censer
or testament of holy loves.
Maybe that will come with time:
now I feel simple gratitude
for being taken in and in and in.

Don't think I mean it less because I said metaphor.
Can't you tell how I love that shape,
that song in the language, metaphor?
grain in a thumb-print for longing,

memory in cirrus or barley,
fright in driftwood—metaphor—
that has always let me in
as she has let me in.

Dear focus of silence
beyond the last space in which to cut
the human shapes of welcome,
mystery past but inviting metaphor,
thank you most tonight for this song,
but also for that yearning in Adam's head
that tore a rag from the floor of his mouth
to be a tongue for me
to wrap around this song,
passage, lintel, carriage light,
for participation, and ignorance,
and at last for perfect worthiness.

TO THE VISITOR

Both ways are down from Times Square,
the distance you have to go
from childhood.

It's Gregory Corso, almost fifty, saying
      Listen—if I don't fuck three times a day
      I get like a tightness here, man,
      like a steel band or something—no shit—
      right across my head,

stones choking the well,
heraldries of cash,
air that makes brazil nuts
taste like urine,

and Johnny Carson, for Christ's sake,
telling Truman Capote a thing or two,
the long way down to go.

NAME

Did I half believe or all the sister
who said I'd been left on the step,
having been kidnapped somewhere by gypsies,
but eyes too dark even for gypsies,
therefore left? or that
any time they might be back
to claim me for the sign in my eyes
of vagrancy? how dark I thought?

Junk the turning wheel and axle-tree,
the kettles junking hung from twine,
junking and saying gypsy Roland,
or foundling or poet in the name,
Oliver and pointing home
and Charlemagne the uncle.

PASSOVER 1974

After crossing the sea at Passover,
he gave more fish, more bread.
His sign is icthus, fish,
and he was bread for centuries,
the fish between our lips
and the blue air in goodbye.

In Cana the gift was so the pair could do
a thing that swims beyond them,
bread for our first communion: wine,
to say the blue air like the ocean
marries us,
to say the fish moves in the ocean,
breathing air,
to say the farmer planting grain
looks up to hear the fish wind,
Christ himself, leaven and green,
like yeast off the ocean,
fish meal and wine of marrow.

WHEEL

She and my daughter at the wheel
making an ordinary cup (for me)
gather with the clay into
the whirlpooling in and down
to the center of clay
and against that drying earth—
my friend and daughter pulled away—
I stare and darken.

She calls this part throwing it—
which sounds easy—
and which means
from a handful of clay
to make a standing space,
the eloquent steady gesture of hands
making a shape to drink,
and it looks easy.

That's a clue because,
though you might not do as well
the first time as my eight year old,
it *is* easy, once you know how.
So metaphors, journeymen to everything,
in the clay's wet shape of palms.
But I try and do tell myself
that making a shape against death
is at least as harmless as making a poem
and as much less poor
as I am able to drink from it.

Put on the high tough glazes,
fire until it answers,
in blue and surface bite,
the sound—ceramic—
and it will cool
in infinite regress
until some night
of a cloud's slow shoulder roll
against the invisibly wet and wheeling moon.

AND MORNING IN

On a fence post the rooster simply
saying to the sun our father
hello old cock I'm up again
and so are you